GEORGE WASHINGTON

The Founding Father of the US Constitution

Written by Mélanie Mettra
In collaboration with Antoine Baudry
Translated by Carly Probert

History 50MINUTES.com

GEORGE WASHINGTON

KEY INFORMATION

- **Birth:** 22 February 1732 in Pope's Creek (Virginia)
- **Death:** 14 December 1799 in Mount Vernon (Virginia)
- **Political party:** Leaned towards Hamiltonian federalism
- **Election dates:**
  - 4 February 1789, first term
  - 13 February 1793, second term
- **Office term:** 7 years
- **Main contributions:**
  - The US Constitution
  - The implementation of federal power and the presidential function
  - Diplomatic protectionism

INTRODUCTION

George Washington, the first president of the United States, is a crucial figure. His name is known by all thanks to the federal capital which bears his name. His face is familiar from the US dollar bills and his statue on Mount Rushmore (South Dakota).

One US dollar bill, 2003.

Recognized as one of the Founding Fathers of the United States of America, he participated in the birth of a nation. From the Seven Years' War against the French (1756-1763) and the War of Independence against the British (1775-1783), to the definition of American protectionism, the drafting of the Constitution for the creation of federal government bodies, he was at the heart of the values and identity of the country, which still benefits from his legacy today. Deeply engaged in his time, he was faced with the emergence of major issues in the history of the United States, both internal, such as relations with the Native Americans and the issue of slavery, and external, such as diplomatic policy with Europe.

BIOGRAPHY

George Washington by Gilbert Stuart, 1797.

YOUTH

George Washington was born on 22 February 1732 in Pope's Creek in Westmoreland Country in the state of Virginia. His father, Augustine Washington c. 1694-1743), a planter, had three children from a previous marriage. After being widowed in 1729, he remarried two years later to Mary Ball (1708-1789), with whom he had George Washington, their eldest son. On the death of his father, he only inherited a small amount of land, most of it having been left to his half-brothers. It was one of these siblings, Lawrence Washington (1718-1752), who supported the education of young George at the age of 11. An average student, he stopped his schooling at 15 and became a surveyor engineer. With his income, he bought land located mainly in Western Virginia. In 1752, he inherited property in Mount Vernon from his half-brother Lawrence, becoming a wealthy landowner. He also replaced Lawrence as a commander of the militia of Virginia.

While Franco-British relations in the US were deteriorating, the governor of Virginia, Robert Dinwiddie (1693-1770), sent the new lieutenant-colonel to the Ohio Valley, where the French had erected a military building, Fort Duquesne. Responsible for building a British fort (Fort Necessity) to face that of the French and clearing the area that is present-day Pittsburgh, he took part in a brief confrontation in which his men killed the French commander Joseph Coulon de Jumonville (1718-1754) in strange circumstances. This was the first serious incident in a war that would see the British and the French fight against each other for seven years in the Americas. During the conflict, George Washington served as an officer and stood out particularly when taking Fort Duquesne in 1758. He was then appointed colonel.

The English take possession of Fort Duquesne, 25 November 1758.

In 1759, once the Ohio Valley was taken back from the British and the Franco-British war had ended, he retired to his estate in Mount Vernon, where he married a rich widow, Martha Dandridge Custis (1731-1802), thus increasing his land capital. He was now the owner of hundreds of hectares of tobacco plantations and fisheries on the Potomac River, operated by more than one hundred slaves.

POLITICAL CAREER

A Virginian aristocrat, he was a member of the House of Burgesses in Virginia between 1759 and 1774. Undergoing rules, taxes and trade monopolies imposed by the British, he quickly became one of the leaders in the fight against British colonial policy. In 1774 and 1775, he was elected the representative of Virginia in the first and second Continental Congress, where he participated in the drafting and adoption of the Declaration of Independence on 4 July 1776. Appointed Commander in Chief of the Continental Army in June 1775, he reorganized the undisciplined troops and engaged in the war against the British, who were forced to evacuate Boston on 17 March 1776. Despite a defeat in New York in September 1776 and a difficult winter in Pennsylvania, he managed to keep up the morale of his troops by winning important victories: those of Trenton and Princeton in January 1777 and that of Philadelphia, abandoned by the British in 1778. On 19 October 1781, supported by the French troops commanded by Jean-Baptiste Donatien de Rochambeau (1725-1807), he finally forced the British General Charles Cornwallis (1738-1805) to surrender at Yorktown.

Once peace was restored, George Washington was quick to return once again to his estate in Mount Vernon. However, the dysfunctions of the young confederation led him to return to the political scene. He accepted the presidency of the Philadelphia Constitutional Convention in 1787, which wrote, under his guidance, the new Constitution of the 13 federal states. He was elected first president of the United States after the formation of the new government.

During his two terms, he worked to build the legislative and administrative tools of the young American nation, launched an economic policy which was heavily influenced by Hamiltonian federalism and laid the foundations for a new diplomacy, marked by his wish for neutrality towards his former French and British opponents.

In 1796, disappointed and tired of the increasingly significant political disagreements that appeared within his own government, he retired to Mount Vernon again. He enjoyed only three years of retirement before dying of a throat infection on 14 December 1799, at the age of 67.

POLITICAL, SOCIAL AND ECONOMIC CONTEXT

THE BRITISH COLONIES AND THEIR INHABITANTS

1620 saw the arrival of Anglo-Saxon migrants in North America, who came looking for land to exploit and a place of freedom and equality. This phenomenon was so significant that, in the 18th century, the East Coast territories became colonies under the rule of King George III of England (1738-1820), and included almost two million inhabitants in the mid-1760s.

The economy of the northern colonies – which included Massachusetts, New Hampshire, New York, Pennsylvania, New Jersey, Delaware and Maryland – were characterized by the wood business, medium-sized polyculture farms and proto-industrialization based on shipbuilding, distillation and spinning. The population, mainly composed of wealthy merchants and marked by a strong Protestant Puritanism, gathered in large cities such as Philadelphia, New York, Boston and Baltimore.

The southern colonies – which included Virginia, North Carolina, South Carolina and Georgia – were, in turn, specialized in the operation of tobacco, rice, indigo and cotton, all in immense quantities. The cities and ports were less developed than in the north. Virginia, the home of the future President George Washington, was the most populous colony, where, like in Georgia and Carolina, an aristocracy of wealthy planters could be found. Pillars of the agricultural economy, especially in the south where people grew cotton and tobacco, slaves represented nearly 30% of the population in the 1760s. Their condition divided society from the late 17th century, driven notably by the Quakers (Protestant religious community) of Pennsylvania, who were in favor of the abolition of slavery. A society for the emancipation of Free Blacks was also created in the 1770s in Philadelphia. Through the establishment of primary schools for black Americans, it promoted the education and emancipation of slaves. Through such initiatives, the northern states gradually abolished slavery: Vermont in 1777, Pennsylvania in 1780, Virginia in 1782 and Massachusetts in 1783. At the end of the 18th century, slavery was banned throughout the north of the Federation, but the 1788 Constitution did not take it into account and did not include this in its text.

Along the western border of the British colonies were Native American territories. From the beginning, the first colonization wave of migrants clashed with the inhabitants already living there. First taken as models for the exploitation of America's resources, the Native Americans soon became a permanent threat because of their opposition to the colonization of their lands. There were numerous clashes between them and the settlers, which ended either with the confiscation of their land by force or through treaties. Thus the agreement of Fort Stanwix (1768) confirmed the cessation of the Iroquois territory in Ohio to the British in exchange for the land in the colony of New York. To achieve their aims, the British did not hesitate to use unorthodox stratagems. For example, during the Battle of Point Pleasant in 1774 (West Virginia town), they distributed blankets infected with smallpox, contaminating thousands of Native Americans. In 1779, George Washington, then commander of the Continental Army during the Revolutionary War, ordered the conquest of the Iroquois territory, a tribe that was allied with the British at the time. In 1784, with the second Treaty of Fort Stanwix, the Shawnee (Native American people) ceded their lands to the east and south of Ohio. In July 1787, the Northwest Ordinance opened for settlement territories within the region, while prohibiting the abusive appropriation of the land without the permission of their Native American owners. However, this clause was frequently disobeyed, sparking the revolt of the dispossessed nations who did not hesitate to fight back, as was the case with the Miamis tribe of the leader Little Turtle (c. 1752-1812), who inflicted heavy losses on the Americans, first in 1790, then in 1791 at the Battle of the Wabash. In 1794, it was the federal armies who were victorious at Fallen Timbers, allowing for the installation of settlers on the territories of the Northwest Ordinance, such as those from Appalachia, Mississippi and Tennessee. These Indian Wars punctuated the 18th and 19th centuries.

Chief Little Turtle.

The Northwest Ordinance, passed by the US Congress on 13 July 1787, recognized the Native American tribes as foreign nations, with whom it was necessary to establish a treaty before conquering their territory. It also established the rules for the creation of a new state and its entry in the Union. Thus, the territories must have 60 000 inhabitants to access the statehood, a requirement that actually promoted territorial conquest and the implantation of settlers in the new land to achieve this privileged status. The Northwest Ordinance also raised dissension about slavery, which it prohibited, increasing the differences between the northern and southern states.

FRENCH AND INDIAN WAR

Far from the American continent, the major European powers entered into a conflict in 1756 that would have a global impact, called the Seven Years' War, fought between the Archduchy of Austria and the Kingdom of Prussia, and also the British against the French. The war had its roots in the previous war, called the "Austrian Succession" (1740-1748), during which the Prussians took over the Austrian Silesia. In January 1756, King George II of England (1683-1760) signed a neutrality agreement with the Kingdom of Prussia, while the France of Louis XV (1710-1774) and the Austria of Maria Theresa (1717-1780) joined forces. The war raged in Europe, but also in the colonies. Indeed, the French held vast territories on the American continent, such as New France (i.e. the basins of Mississippi and Missouri, as well as the Great Lakes, Canada, Acadia and part of Louisiana) that formed the arc of a circle that went from the far north to the Gulf of Mexico, enclosing the British colonies. Such a territory was bound to create rivalries between the French and the British, who competed for a long time to obtain dominance over these regions and the access and exploitation of their resources. In the early 1750s, tensions were rising in the Ohio Valley.

Thus, in 1754, the troops of George Washington, commissioned by the Governor of Virginia, patrolled the area of Fort Duquesne with the intention of building a fort to face their opponents. But the French commander was killed in a clash, in unclear circumstances. This event triggered a war known as the French and Indian War by the British (also called the "War of Conquest") because of the support given by some Native American (known at the time as Indian) tribes to the French. The battles took place across the entire US territory. In July 1754, the French won the first victory in Pennsylvania, at the Battle of Fort Necessity. In 1758, the British troops, aided by those of George Washington, took Fort Duquesne, ending French rule in the lands of Ohio.

In the province of New York, the French troops led by General Louis Joseph de Montcalm (1712-1759) won the successive victories of Fort Henry and Fort Carillon in 1757 and 1758.

The Victory of Montcalm's Troops at Carillon, by Henry Alexander Ogden, beginning of 20th century.

In New France, Charles Lawrence (1709-1760), Governor of Nova Scotia, organized the deportation of the French population of Acadia in June 1755, as they refused to pledge the allegiance and he feared they would take up arms against him. In June 1759, the city of Quebec suffered the siege and bombardment of the naval forces of the British General James Wolfe (1727-1759). After two months of uncertainty, on 13 September the Franco-British troops clashed on the Plains of Abraham, where the generals of the two armies, Briton James Wolfe and the French Louis-Joseph de Montcalm were killed. Quebec surrendered on

16 September 1759. On 8 September 1760, Montreal signed its surrender, and with it came the end of New France, which was now British property.

Death of General Wolfe, by Benjamin West, 1770.

On 10 January 1763, the Treaty of Paris put an end to the

Seven Years' War, as well as most of the French colonies in North America, which were ceded to the British.

THE DECLARATION AND WAR OF INDEPENDENCE

After the victory against the French, the English King George III reasserted his power in the British colonies. He reinforced the exclusive trade policy that bound them with the metropolis, hardened the repression of fraud against the heavy taxes imposed by the Crown (on tea, sugar, the press, etc.) and limited the influence of the Assemblies, by making the governors depend on the Crown for remuneration. Soon, the Americans refused this colonialist pressure imposed by a parliament in which they had no representatives, despite their claims. They then took action to boycott British goods, in 1767 and 1768, which was severely punished by the Townshend Acts that imposed hefty customs charges from the colonies to obtain the money needed to finance the colonial administration. These measures led to sometimes violent uprisings, like the Boston Massacre (5 March 1770), during which British soldiers fired on the crowd, or the Boston Tea Party of 16 December 1773, which saw the destruction of the tea shipments in retaliation against the monopoly held by the East India Company on the sale of tea in America. Great Britain immediately reacted through what would later be called the Intolerable Acts, punitive laws that ruined the commerce of Boston by ordering the closure of the port and put an end to the freedoms granted to Massachusetts. Faced with repression, the settlements came together and met in Philadelphia in

1774, during a Continental Congress initiated by Benjamin Franklin (American philosopher, physicist and statesman, 1706-1790).

During the Boston Tea Party the colonists – some dressed as Native Americans – destroyed a tea shipment sent by the East India Company by throwing the tea into Boston Harbor.

In June 1775, as the second Continental Congress was opening, a first battle was fought between the British and the Americans, in which George Washington played a part as the commander of the first Continental Army. While on 4 July 1776, the 13 insurgent states adopted the Declaration of Independence and ratified, on 15 November 1777, the articles of the Confederation, the War of Independence raged on. Some Americans (the "Loyalists") remained loyal to the British, who hired foreign mercenaries to support their armies against the few troops, poorly organized and trained in haste, of George Washington. The Continental Army was first held in check by the forces of the former colonial power, as in the defeat of New York in 1776 and that of Philadelphia a year later. However, the insurgents quickly rallied the European opponents of Britain to their cause. Through the diplomatic mission of Benjamin Franklin, France first saw this as an opportunity to take revenge after the defeat of the Seven Years' War and the loss of its colonies. General Lafayette (1757-1834) and Count Jean-Baptiste Donatien de Rochambeau (1725-1807) took the lead of the French army and participated alongside George Washington in the victory of Yorktown. The capitulation of Lord Charles Cornwallis (British Governor General of India, 1738-1805) precipitated the end of the War of Independence. The Peace of Paris, signed on 3 September 1783, recognized the new federated Republic of the United States.

THE BIRTH OF A NATION

After the proclamation of the United States Declaration of Independence on 4 July 1776, the 13 former British colonies declared themselves sovereign states. From 1777, they attempted to draft the Articles of Confederation to govern this covenant, but the many divisions, including trade and customs, led to acrimonious debates. Indeed, the future federal government would have no power in financial matters: it could not impose any taxes, and its resources were only provided by the free contribution of the member states. A new Convention was therefore held in May 1787 at the initiative of the state of Virginia, under the chairmanship of its representative, George Washington.

For four months, it worked on creating a text that preserved state autonomy, while defining and affirming the federal government's powers. The draft Constitution was adopted on 17 September 1787, and came into effect on 4 March 1789, at the dawn of the mandate of the first president of the United States.

HIGHLIGHTS

A UNANIMOUSLY CHOSEN PRESIDENT

The first presidential election in February 1789 was not an election in the traditional sense. The Members of Congress who participated in the drafting of the Constitution, in which the status of the president was defined, were required to designate the leader of the new federation. However, there was no real opposition, and the 11 candidates running did not offer a very defined program, nor were their programs very distinct from one another. Therefore, only the skills and experience of the candidates were taken into account in this election.

Each state had the same number of electors and representatives in Congress. Given the novelty of the system, their appointment, which may or may not have been subject to a popular vote, was sometimes risky. Thus, the state of New York failed to gather a great elector that year. Moreover, of the 81 that were theoretically supposed to vote, only 69 took part. Each had two ballots, one for electing the president and another for electing the vice president. The candidate who received the highest number of votes would access the top legislature, and the second would receive the vice-presidency. George Washington was unanimously elected with 69 votes and John Adams (1735-1826) was appointed vice president with 34 votes.

The 1792 election, which led to George Washington being chosen for a second term, unfolded somewhat differently.

Firstly, the electors were all in attendance. With the new states entered into the Union, they totaled 132. Then, the first oppositions appeared, as well as two schools of thought:

- The first, led by the Secretary of the Treasury, Alexander Hamilton (1757-1804), was oriented towards federalism limiting the power of states;
- The second, led by Thomas Jefferson (1743-1826), the Secretary of State for Foreign Affairs, instead advocated the autonomy of states in a Republican-Democratic Party.

Although he was unwilling to run for a second term, George Washington was strongly encouraged to do so. Even though he was more inclined towards federalism, the members of both parties deemed him to be the only one able to overcome their differences. He was therefore unanimously re-elected against the other four candidates, with the incumbent Vice President John Adams also pursuing his mandate. However, it should be noted that the participation rate was very low: only between 1% and 2% of the population participated.

DID YOU KNOW?

The first two American presidential elections had yet to specify a legislative framework regarding the designation of his great electors. Each state was free to decide on the voting system, of which there were many variations. The great electors were sometimes designated by the states parliament, sometimes by the citizens, or parliament could choose among the candidates who were most popular among the voters.

A FEDERALIST POLICY

The Constitution came into effect when George Washington began his presidential term. It provided for both the maintaining of the independence of the 13 states that constituted the 1789 United States of America, and an important federal power. Throughout his two terms, President George Washington worked to define and develop the bodies and organs of this form of government and its constitutional and legislative basis, as new states progressively joined the federation (Vermont in 1791, Kentucky in 1792 and Tennessee in 1796).

The first major contribution of George Washington as the first president of the United States was the Bill of Rights, adopted in 1789 and ratified by the Congress in December 1791. The bill aimed to reassure the citizens who feared that the powers conferred by the Constitution to the central government would restrict individual freedoms, containing ten amendments to protect the freedom of speech, press, religion, assembly, the carrying of weapons, protection in the face of justice, etc.

In the economic sphere, the policy of George Washington was strongly marked by Hamiltonian thinking. Within his government, his two principal secretaries of state defended somewhat different conceptions of federalism. Although

Alexander Hamilton, Secretary of the Treasury, defended the idea of an aristocratic republic whose enlightened government would preserve general interest in the face of popular pressure, Thomas Jefferson, Secretary of State for Foreign Affairs, advocated the limitation of the prerogatives of the central power and the widest possible independence for the states, focusing on individual freedoms and control of the government by the people.

The early work of Alexander Hamilton as Secretary of the Treasury was the reorganization of budgetary affairs. First, on 22 September 1789, the Treasury department was instituted, responsible for leading the federal government's economic policy. The financing of the state's debts by the federal government was then introduced. Indeed, the 13 federated states and the continental government went into heavy debt during the War of Independence, causing a serious budget crisis.

In order to repay the debts and prove the strength of the young nation to its creditors, the federal government was now able, thanks to the new Constitution, to fix and collect taxes on US international trade, as well as regulate it. Customs duties were therefore the main source of federal revenue, the latter being used for debt repayment. Through the acts of 4 and 5 August 1790, the state's debt was natio-nalized and the country was bailed out. On 25 February 1791, the first bank of the United States was founded to improve the financial situation and to ensure smooth economic operation. On 2 April 1792, the Coinage Act endorsed the creation of a mint to make the new federal currency: the US dollar.

On the judicial level, George Washington signed the Judiciary Act in 1789, which was the basis for new judicial institutions. A supreme court was created, headed by a senior judge, assisted initially by five assessors, appointed by the President and approved by the Congress.

EXPANDING BORDERS

In 1789, the United States consisted of 13 states along the East Coast. To the west, a vast territory occupied by British settlers and Native American nations separated them from the colony of Louisiana and the Kingdom of New Spain, which brought together the Spanish land. Also Spanish, Florida bordered the new nation to the south. Throughout the 18th and 19th centuries, these territories would be the subject of revolts and negotiations.

The financial windfall that represented the sale of territories that were considered "virgin land" and the conditions for creating a new state specified by the Northwest Ordinance of 1787 led a number of pioneers to extend the US western frontier. However, the British still held forts and territories there. To protect these territories, they combined with the Native American populations who were also struggling to protect their land, particularly in Ohio.

The position of George Washington regarding the Native Americans was twofold. He condemned the raids organized by American conquerors wishing to set up in their territories. Indeed, against those he considered to be savages, he recommended the use of treaties and advocated the "civilization" of these indigenous populations through education, financial and material support. Nevertheless, he did not hesitate to severely punish Native American uprisings, as in the clashes against the indigenous nations of the Ohio River in 1791 and 1794, which ended with the Treaty of Greenville in 1795. The Native Americans then ceded the lands of Ohio, Michigan and Indiana to the government. The same year, the British left the forts that they still held in the region. But every new advance westwards led to clashes, which would carry on for over a century.

To the south, the Treaty of San Lorenzo (or Pinckney), signed on 27 October 1795 between Spain and the United States, attributed authority over the territory east of Mississippi to the Confederation, thereby opening the river and the port of New Orleans to the commercial movement of US ships. In return, the Spaniards maximized the tax efficiency of the region, which was in full economic expansion, through the cultivation of cotton.

In 1789, the US capital was New York. The Congress moved to Philadelphia in December 1790, located halfway between New York and Virginia, and became the provisional capital. Indeed, the Constitution planned for the creation of a new capital on neutral ground to halt the competition between the States wishing to host it. Chosen by the Residence Act of July 1790 on the banks of the Potomac in northern Virginia, the latter ceded in March 1791, along with the state of Maryland, an area of about 250 square kilometers, which made up the new District of Columbia. The French architect Pierre Charles l'Enfant (1754-1825) was in charge of establishing the plans for the city that would later be named after the first president of the United States. The first brick of the White House was laid in 1792, of the Capitol in 1793.

INTERNATIONAL RELATIONS

After the Seven Years' War and the War of Independence, the diplomatic international relations of the young American nation were not easy.

When the French Revolution broke out in 1789, the French people, who had supported the Americans in their own revolution –Gilbert du Mortier de La Fayette participated in the final victory of the US troops at Yorktown, alongside George Washington – received favor with the American public. But when the Anglo-French war broke out in 1793, politicians were divided. The clashes with the British, who raised Native American nations to seek their support in the western territories, motivated some of them to back Secretary of State Thomas Jefferson to support a US intervention in France's favor. Others, supportive of the Secretary of the Treasury Alexander Hamilton, who was anxious to maintain the privileged links with Britain, were reluctant to get involved. George Washington, bypassing the rival factions, chose a policy of neutrality (statement from 22 April 1793), which would be put to the test due to maneuvers from both the French and the British.

In early April 1793, the first Ambassador of the French Republic, Edmond-Charles Genet (1763-1834), arrived in South Carolina, in charge of asking for help from the United States President. Before even meeting him and, subsequently, despite the proclamation of neutrality, he took advantage of his popularity to arm four warships and raise militias. Angered by this behavior, George Washington, after a severe reprimand which was ignored by Edmond-Charles Genet, called on France to withdraw his mandate. Therefore, instead of consolidating the Franco-American relations, the French ambassador caused their relationship to deteriorate. This relationship was completely destroyed in 1797 by the Directory.

The British were not far behind. In 1793, Britain announced that it would seize all vessels trading with France, even those bearing the American flag, which revived the tensions between Britain and the United States. George Washington immediately suspended maritime trade and launched the construction of three warships. He still tried to obtain reconciliation with the British, but they multiplied provocations by continuing to build forts to the west of federated states and pushing the Native American nations to rebel in favor of their own cause. However, George Washington managed, through diplomacy and his envoy, John Jay (1745-1829), to negotiate a treaty (the Treaty of London) which was ratified in October 1795. The British then agreed to leave the forts they still occupied and to compensate the US commercial ships, in return for the commercial status of a privileged nation.

Despite these numerous difficulties, George Washington strived to maintain his policy of neutrality, which he reaffirmed in his farewell speech. At the end of his second term, while his government was plagued by many divisions, he was encouraged to stand for election again, but George Washington decided to end his political career. On 20 September 1796, he delivered his final speech in office, in which he reiterated the need for neutrality and unity, announcing the protectionism that would govern US foreign policy until the Second World War (1939-1945).

IMPACT

POLITICAL

In the years following the end of George Washington's term, the political and economic face of the United States continued to bear his mark. The divisions that had emerged during his two terms between supporters of the political vision of Alexander Hamilton and those who favored Thomas Jefferson grew further under the presidency of John Adams (1797-1801). Although, like his predecessor, he attempted to govern beyond the partisan struggles, his international policy favored Jeffersonian views. With George Washington failing to maintain his apolitical perception of government, it was under his presidency that bipartisanship was born, which would mark the coming centuries: the Federalists inspired the future Republican Party, while the Republican Democrats would be at the origin of the Democratic Party.

Meanwhile, the economy was deeply anchored in the industrialization of the north and finance. Promoting the emergence of a new economy based on industry and monetary and stock exchanges, George Washington was also launching the great adventure of American banking, public and private, which was not particularly successful afterwards. The first federal bank was replaced by a second in 1812, but until 1863, the issuing of currency was not registered. However, the National Bank Act of that year limited the issuance of currency to private banks, whose bills could be charged as federal pension assets. In 1913, the Federal Reserve endorsed the monopoly of issuance of the federal government.

THE AMERICAN CIVIL WAR AND THE CONQUEST OF THE WEST

In the southern states in the 1790s, the challenges of the future American Civil War (1861-1865) emerged. Indeed, the agricultural and planting economy was growing. While it was initially based on the cultivation of tobacco, technical innovations in spinning and the rise in demand favored the cultivation of cotton, which quickly spread from the 1790s. This culture, which required a significant working force, was mainly operated by slaves, whose population was growing: in the second half of the 18th century, they accounted for between a third and a sixth of the total population of the United States. With the advance westward, the new conquered lands were vested in the cultivation of tobacco, cotton and dye plants, which resulted in the displacement of enslaved populations. From the 1770s, several northern states voted for the abolition of slavery, but George Washington, himself a slave owner who nevertheless repeatedly showed abolitionist inclinations, did not make a decision on the subject. He thus left his successors to tackle this thorny issue, which would be settled at the price of a bloody civil war.

It was also under the presidency of George Washington that the great conquest of the West began, the foundation of the American identity. The first agreements with the Native Americans and the Spaniards, obtained by force or through diplomacy, opened the era of pioneers who sought, through the discovery and conquering of new territories in the West, to extend the political, but above all the economic and commercial influence of the young federal nation.

American Progress by John Gast, 1872. This painting represents the Manifest Destiny, showing that American Settlers were destined to move though the continent.

A SOLID CONSTITUTION

Finally, George Washington established the constitutional foundations of the nation, which would still be going strong two centuries later, through the Constitution on which he worked, thanks to the amendments that still govern justice and American liberties today, and thanks to a certain idea of diplomacy and the position of the United States on the world stage, which would only really be challenged with the Second World War – during which the United States broke their isolation.

George Washington was also the one who gave the presidential office its meaning. The representation of the role, duties and position of the head of the federal government was largely inherited from his own actions. It was under his presidency that the tradition of the president choosing the cabinet himself was born, as was the limitation of the exercise of supreme power to two terms and the appointment of a large number of staff by the head of state (ambassadors, judges of the Supreme Court, etc.). While firmly anchoring the executive power represented by the presidential office, he clearly defined the role of the Congress and its legislative power. He was careful to avoid interfering in debates, except in constitutional matters, and did not use his veto power to influence decisions. During the Whiskey Revolt of 1794, he also demonstrated the superiority of federal power over the states, a power that was at first ensured in a rudimentary manner by armed militias, and whose specificity and functions would be developed in the decades that followed.

SUMMARY

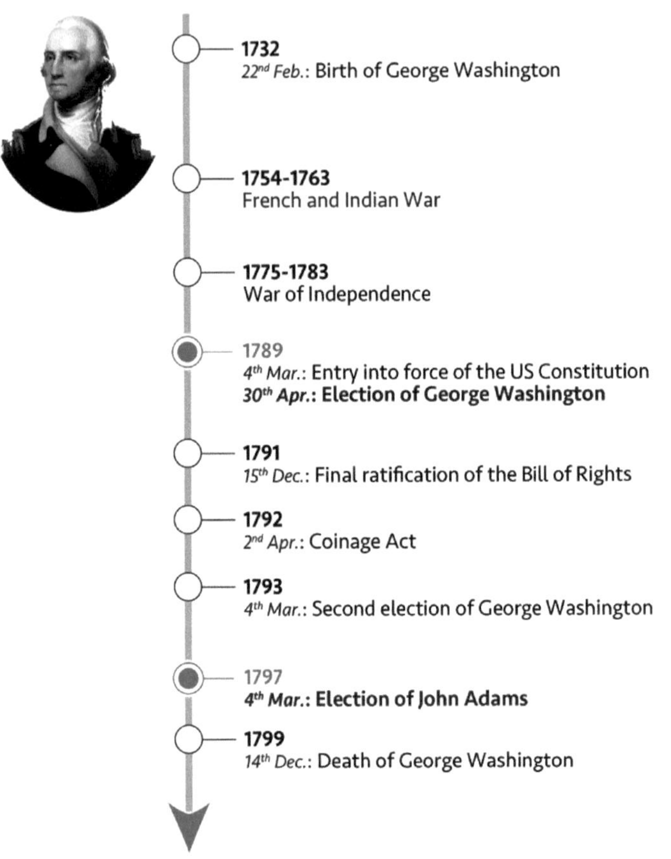

1732
22nd Feb.: Birth of George Washington

1754-1763
French and Indian War

1775-1783
War of Independence

1789
4th Mar.: Entry into force of the US Constitution
30th Apr.: **Election of George Washington**

1791
15th Dec.: Final ratification of the Bill of Rights

1792
2nd Apr.: Coinage Act

1793
4th Mar.: Second election of George Washington

1797
4th Mar.: **Election of John Adams**

1799
14th Dec.: Death of George Washington

- George Washington, appointed colonel by the Governor of Virginia, participated in the Seven Years' War with the British against the French.

- In 1775, he was elected representative of Virginia in the first and second Continental Congress and participated in the Declaration of Independence and that of the Union Acts, the first foundations of the Constitution.
- Between 1775 and 1783, he led the Convention, the outcome of which was the ratified Constitution.
- He led the Continental Army in the war between the newly independent nation and the British settlers.
- Elected the first president of the United States, he passed many founding texts of the American nation: the Bill of Rights, the law on currency (Coinage Act) and the law of judicial functioning (Judiciary Act).
- He therefore laid the foundations of the judicial and financial institutions of the federal state.
- During the conflict between the United States and the European nations (particularly France and Britain), he attempted to establish diplomacy that aimed to respect the neutrality of the American nation.
- Under his tenure, the first political parties and positions began to appear, led by the Secretary of the Treasury, Alexander Hamilton, and the Secretary of State for Foreign Affairs, Thomas Jefferson.
- Despite an inclination to abolitionism and respect for the Native American nations, George Washington did not define a specific policy addressing the issues of slavery and the native territories, which were also not addressed in the Constitution.
- After his two terms and although his government encouraged him to run again, George Washington left the political stage to return to his property, where he died three years later.

We want to hear from you!
Leave a comment on your online library
and share your favourite books on social media!

FIND OUT MORE

BIBLIOGRAPHY

- Alden, J.R. (2011) *The War of the Revolution*. New York: Skyhorse Publishing.
- Bruce, D.K. (1954) *Les présidents des USA de George Washington à Abraham Lincoln*. Paris: Gallimard.
- Cunliffe, M. (2011) *George Washington: Man and Monument*. Whitefish, Montana: Literary Licensing.
- Desbiens, A. (2012) *Histoire des États-Unis. Des origines à nos jours*. Paris: Éditions du Nouveau Monde.
- Kaspi, A. (1972) *La naissance des États-Unis. Révolution ou guerre d'indépendance?* Paris: Presses Universitaires de France.
- Meyer, J. (2009) *L'Europe et la conquête du monde. XVIe-XVII siècles*. Paris: Armand Colin.
- Portes, J. (2010) *Histoire des États-Unis. De 1776 à nos jours*. Paris: Armand Colin.

ADDITIONAL SOURCES

- Brumwell, S. (2012) *George Washington: Gentleman Warrior*. London: Quercus.
- Chernow, R. (2011) *Washington*. London: Penguin.
- Faulkner, H.U. (1943) *American Economic History*, Fifth Edition. New York: Harper and Brothers.
- Ferling, J. (2009) *Almost A Miracle: The American Victory in the War of Independence*. Oxford: Oxford University Press.
- Miller Center (No date) *George Washington (1732-1799).*

[Online]. [Accessed 9 December 2016]. Available from:
<http://millercenter.org/president/washington>

ICONOGRAPHIC SOURCES

- One US dollar bill, series 2003. Royalty-free reproduction picture.
- *George Washington*, by Gilbert Stuart, 1797. Royalty-free reproduction picture.
- The English take possession of Fort Duquesne, 25 November 1758. © Alfred Waud.
- Chief Little Turtle. Royalty-free reproduction picture.
- *The Victory of Montcalm's Troops at Carillon*, painting Henry Alexander Ogden, early 20th century. Royalty-free reproduction picture.
- *Death of general Wolfe* by Benjamin West, 1770 . Royalty free reproduction picture .
- During the Boston Tea Party the colonists – some dressed as Native Americans – destroyed a tea shipment sent by the East India Company by throwing the tea into Boston Harbor. Copy of a lithography by Sarony & Major, 1846. Royalty-free reproduction picture
- *American Progress* by John Gast, 1872. This painting represents the Manifest Destiny, showing that American Settlers were destined to move though the continent. Royalty-free reproduction picture.

DOCUMENTARIES

- *Yorktown 1781*. (1976) [Documentary]. Henri Turenne and Daniel Costelle. Dir. France.

- *10 présidents américains célèbres.* (2012) [Documentary]. Pierre Étienne Pommier. Dir. France.

IMPROVE YOUR GENERAL KNOWLEDGE

IN A BLINK OF AN EYE !

www.50minutes.com

www.50minutes.com

Ebook EAN: 9782806276070

Paperback EAN: 9782806277008

Legal Deposit: D/2016/12603/105

Cover: © Primento

Digital conception by Primento, the digital partner of publishers.